Minecraft: Diary of a Wimpy Zombie

Table of Contents

Zombie Disclaimer

While exploring Minecraft, it is possible for players to come across various Easter eggs hidden in the game. The Diary of a Wimpy Zombie which contains an account of the life of a Minecraft Zombie is not one of them.

While Minecraft focuses on the player's perspective, there is little to no idea about how the other inhabitants of the Minecraft universe fare in the game.

- What do they do?

- How do they spend their days and nights?

- Do they do anything other than just ranging around and hurting players as soon as they see them?

If you have those questions and more, the Diary of a Wimpy Zombie has all the answers you need.

Keep in mind that this isn't a particularly brave Zombie. He's just your average Zombie trying to find meaning and get on with his life.

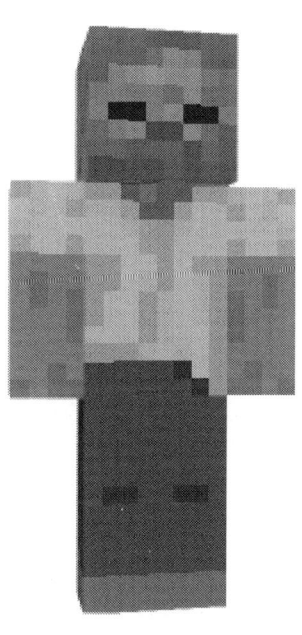

What he encounters on a day to day basis might shock you; or not. We'll let you be the judge of that. Read on and experience life as a zombie.

Real Disclaimer: This account may or may not count as a Minecraft Easter Egg but it is pretty close in terms of rarity.

No Zombies or players were hurt in the telling of this tale.

We've tried to get in touch with Urgel about his diary but we have heard nothing from him so far.

Hello from the Other Side!

So you've probably heard about Minecraft: The game. The one with the blocks that is totally awesome.

Everyone wants to play it. If you haven't played it yet, you still must have heard the Minecraft players talk about it.

"Oh my player is this, my player is that. I built this, I built that"

Some players brag about their kills. Yeah, that's right, you can kill in Minecraft but you can only kill mobs or monsters.

Well let me tell you this. Every time you kill a mob in Minecraft, you hurt someone.

'Who gets hurt?' I hear you asking. Well, you hurt me.

Who am I? My name is Urgel and I am a Minecraft Zombie. That's right, a Zombie. I'm one of the green creatures but I don't explode. Those are Creepers. They're a little weird which might be a bit of an understatement.

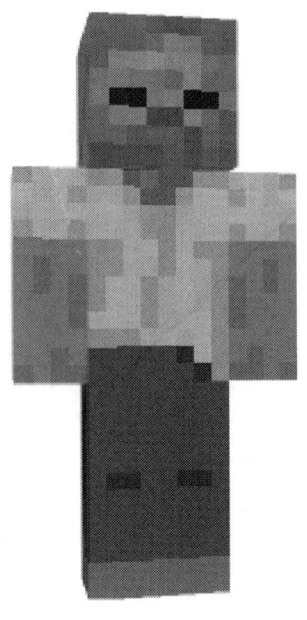

Writing in this diary is my attempt to not only shed some more light on life as a zombie, it's also meant to help me keep track of my days, to be more specific, in Minecraft.

I have also noticed there are a lot of theories about Zombies so I will slowly clear out the misconceptions there are against Zombies. You'll get the tale, straight from the horse's mouth, or in this case, the Zombie's mouth.

So I say, Hello, from the other side.

As I mentioned, my name is Urgel. My hobbies include travelling. I have others but I can't remember them. A faulty memory is part of being a Zombie.

I love to travel and every day is an adventure! I am 1 day old. That's the funny thing about being a Zombie on Minecraft. We don't seem to age but I am fairly young.

Some Zombies do tend to live for 40 or 50 days. There's also talk of ancient Zombies who go up into the mountains and are never seen off but that might just be a story. Zombies living in a cave; it's absurd, right?

Another fun thing about being a Zombie is that if your personal motto is *'Live each day like there's no tomorrow,'* then congratulations!

You just qualified for the position of a Zombie on Minecraft. We're not hiring though.

See, if you're interested in becoming a Zombie then you have to understand that I didn't choose the game, the game life chose me.

Why Do I Feel So Blue When I am Green?

As a Zombie, I am always plagued with the question, such as:

Where did I come from?

Who was I?

What are the glowing lights I see?

They're a little scary and all I have been taught is to stay away from them.

Other Zombies don't question this fact. I know, because I asked them. No one has the answer to this.

They're more than happy, plodding along, doing what they do and living in the moment. But not me; I need to know.

Sometimes, I have dreams about a completely different life but I can't remember them. That's the Zombie faulty memory playing tricks on my mind.

As a Zombie my time is pretty simple, I get to roam the land and sometimes, if I am lucky, ride the animals I come across. I'm a little slow as compared to normal players but faster than most Zombies.

We're a relaxed bunch. We don't like to be quick about things. Contrary to popular belief, we're actually pretty peaceful and quiet.

We don't make a lot of noise, we love to explore and we love nature. That's why we're so green. Yeah, we're one with nature. That's deep. Yet even at our slow pace, time flies quickly.

Sometimes, I get pretty restless though. I don't feel one with nature. I am green yet, inside, I feel so blue.

Wanting to know the answers my tribe could not provide, I set off on my own, to look for the Ancient Zombies.

They're rumored to be 140 days old. Surely they must know something which I don't.

So, I donned my favorite blue pants and my favorite blue shirt.

I want to make an amazing first impression on the Ancient Zombies so I choose ones with nice tattered edges. It's always good to be a little fashion savvy as well.

Each day I travel I don't seem to make much progress.

The vast landscape calls to me and often, I will travel until my feet can't carry me anymore. Bone tired, I collapse with exhaustion.

I don't remember anymore after it but I always come to myself in a little while. I have travelled alone for so long, I am wondering if it was good idea to leave my Zombie tribe. Even a Zombie feels lonely sometimes.

Green is the New Black

Another odd thing I noticed is that it's always dark.

My eyes are accustomed to it but sometimes, I come across something which is so blindingly bright, it terrifies me. It must be the sun I have heard about.

In Zombie school, they taught us that the bright ball in the sky is actually the moon. I like the moon. Its light doesn't hurt my eyes.

But there have also been tales of when a bright ball, called the Sun, appears in the sky too. It is said to be so bright that it dazzles and blinds anyone who sees it.

Yes, we do have Zombie school which is usually just a bunch of Zombies, sitting in a circle and the Zombie elders tell us stories.

They're not ordinary ones though; these have been passed down from the Ancient Zombies.

There must be a kernel of truth in them, somewhere. The bright flashes I see sometimes make me wonder if I have found the sun.

My curiosity compels me to go nearer but I am afraid. What if I do burn my eyes out?

Zombies are naturally attracted to black. Our days are dark, our eyes our dark, we see better when it's dark and even the places we search for are dark.

Yeah, as a Zombie you learn pretty early, black is the new green and green is the new black. What does that mean? You'll have to go to Zombie school to find out.

Jeepers and Creepers

I lost track of the days I have been away from the tribe. I have managed pretty well. A neat thing about being a Zombie is that you don't get hungry pretty often.

Yet, I sometimes experience hunger pangs which do

not go away if I eat mushrooms or other resources.

Eating animals satiates my hunger but, at times, the craving is too strong. I don't know what I crave.

I wish I had stayed in my tribe longer to find out. I still experience the flashes where I collapse and remember nothing. It doesn't matter though.

My Zombie elders told me I am nomadic and maybe, destined to be one of the Ancients but sometimes I wonder if they only said that as a means of getting rid of me.

Zombies are social creatures and we travel and live in packs at times. There is safety in numbers and we get to eat well too. I don't know what we hunt though.

I never joined the pack hunts but I remember the meat tasted better than the cows, sheep or pigs I kill and eat.

This nagging hunger and the loneliness are at times too much for me to handle.

Luckily one day, I stumbled upon two other monsters, Sal and Calcium.

Sal is a skeleton I met in the forest. He was lurking behind a tree shooting at the bright, glowing light when I met him.

I cautioned Sal to get away and he agreed to come as long as I tell him what the lights are. I told him all I knew but he had a pretty different tale to tell.

Skeletons are different from Zombies so it's natural they have different stories and to his knowledge, the light hides something. Their eyes are better than ours too.

"I see a shadow sometimes, lurking behind the brightness and if you're not faster than them, they shoot you. You either hunt them or are hunted by them." That was a pretty grim fact for me.

Sal is pretty cool though. He has a crossbow he found lying around and he's good with it too. For arrows, he uses his own bones.

Since they always grow back, I think that's pretty resourceful.

"Come with me,' I asked Sal. "I am looking for the Ancient Zombies. There is a lot I want to find out and I don't have all the answers."

Sal agreed to come since he also experiences the

exhausting moments where he just collapses.

He also seems to have the Zombie faulty memory gene which is odd. Looks like we both have some questions which need answers.

Calcium is a Creeper. He's really odd. Among all the mobs you come across, the Creeper is the one you can never rely on.

They're un-predictable, explode at the slightest provocation and they're very, very clingy. Oh my god.

Once Calcium saw Sal and me, he crept up, hissed at us and tagged along. Creepers don't talk much but they are very stubborn. There's no saying no to a Creeper.

In many ways, they're harmless too. Calcium has wolf-dog like tendencies. He's fierce, loyal and scouts ahead to let us know the path we're following.

Plus having a creeper on board means no one wants to mess with you. Creepers are scary and many mobs will give you a wide berth once they see one with you.

All in all, I like my new posse. I am not lonely anymore and Sal and Calcium actually make me laugh.

When Creepers Lose It

It hadn't been many days with Sal and Calcium before disaster struck us. Calcium was very agitated that day. All of us were a little jumpy because we were travelling across some plains.

Plains don't have trees you can hide behind and unless there are certain hills breaking up the landscape, you can't hide anywhere.

Although I don't know what we need to hide from, it is natural, almost instinctive to want some sort of protection around you.

Besides when you spend so much time in the forests or jungles, plains seem very open.

Sal and I were also on edge but Calcium was a little too agitated. He kept darting back and forth and hissing randomly at things.

I was tempted to scold some sense into Calcium but

Sal told me to leave him alone. He did have a point;

an agitated Creeper is a dangerous Creeper.

We were all climbing down from a hill when we saw

a small house in the distance.

There were no bright lights around but you could still see someone working on it. While I'm always cautious, curiosity got the best of me and even Calcium was intrigued by it.

Sal didn't agree to come closer but he promised to provide cover with his crossbow. He crept closer with us and once he was sure he was close enough, he stopped.

Calcium and I crept closer to get a look but Calcium seemed to be getting more frantic.

I was just thinking of turning back when Calcium started running towards the structure, hissing furiously.

The player who was building the house saw us and ran inside, closing the door but Creepers are stubborn.

Calcium kept running and as soon as he reached the door, he let out an extra loud hiss. I was running right behind Calcium, trying to stop him but as soon as I heard the last hiss, I understood.

I skidded to a stop, dropped down and covered my ears. I knew what would happen next. Calcium exploded.

In Zombie School, they tell us that Creepers explode when they become agitated enough.

The one thing a Creeper hates more than anything in the world are buildings or structures of any kind.

Creepers are huge nature lovers. Give them mountains, open terrains and lush forests, unblemished, untouched and they are happy.

Once they see these structures, their anger at the toll it takes on nature makes them crazy.

Creepers are green in color but they are not like Zombies; they are truly one with nature.

They can't help it. Their stubbornness combined with their anger makes them volatile. I had heard about it before but this was the first time I had seen something like this happen.

Sticks and Stones DO Break My Bones!

After Calcium exploded, I got up and looked at the spot with horror in my eyes. There was a huge gaping hole where the door was.

Inside I could see someone lying on the ground but there was no sign of Calcium.

I looked around but I wasn't sure if I could see Sal. I got up and walked inside. The figure I thought I had seen on the ground was nowhere to be seen.

I went inside the broken door and someone whacked me over the head with a wooden stick. Angry and hurt I retreated only to have a sword pointed at my face.

But I was gaping in surprise at the person who did that. Dressed in similar jeans and a t-shirt, this person was not a Zombie.

Their jeans weren't even ripped and frayed but I was completely surprised. I kept staring like an idiot until the person whacked me on the arm.

That hurt really badly. I wasn't sure if I broke

something or not but luckily, Sal let loose an arrow

and it hit the player in the shoulder.

He fell back, his wooden sword falling to the floor. In anger, I picked it up and stepped inside after him.

You know how Zombie adults tell you that saying about sticks and stones. It's something like this: 'Sticks and stones *may* break my bones....'

Well guess what? Sticks and stones DO break bones and I am not a nice Zombie when I am angry.

The player retrieved another sword and swiped at me but I ducked and bit him.

As I bit him and tasted his flesh, I became frenzied

as I recognized that beautiful, delectable taste.

This was what I had been craving. This was what I was searching for.

I chomped down eagerly while the player succumbed to the bites. Zombies look docile but don't let that fool you. Our barks are not worse than our bites.

The Sun and I – My Final Good Bye

I don't know where Sal ran off to but I didn't realize that he was missing until I was finished with the meal.

I looked around but there was no sign of him. I walked away from the structure, feeling both full and weirdly empty.

So many questions seemed to be answered yet I still needed the advice of the Ancients. I felt full of energy and could see the mountains in the distance.

I picked up my pace and walked faster. Without Sal and Calcium, I was making good time but I missed them, particularly Calcium's wolf-dog habits.

After trekking for what seemed like ages, the mountains where finally within reach.

I clambered up, slowly but made good progress. I could see a dark opening in the side.

It was the cave. I knew, felt it in my bones that this was the cave of the Ancient Zombies.

As I was clambering up though, I felt like the darkness was getting lighter.

I didn't pay much attention to it but slowly, it became apparent. While I was still too naïve, I thought 'Oh my god, this cave is magical.'

Little did I know; those were the early rays of sunlight. It was dawn. I heard painful screams from behind me but just as suddenly, I also heard a voice calling out from the cave.

"You are almost there, don't look down."

Of course, just as soon as I heard that, I couldn't help it, I looked down and the sight filled me with horror.

From the height I was at, I could see Zombies,

Skeletons and Creepers, smoking and then bursting

into flames. In pain, they ran around burning.

The sun's rays were getting stronger and I could feel my skin smoking as well.

Before I could join the fate of my brothers though,

strong, Zombie hands reached out and grasped me.

They pulled me into the cool shade of the cave and the Zombie said, "Welcome, we are the Ancient Zombies. Do you seek anything from us?"

All I did was shake my head to say no. All my questions had been answered. I have seen what few Zombies get to see.

Made in the USA
Middletown, DE
09 December 2016